AWAKEN THE SUPER ACHIEVER WITHIN YOU

HOW TO DEFY THE ODDS AND BETTER YOUR LIFE

MANFRED GWUNIREAMA

ISBN: 978-1-9996642-7-5

First Published by:

KINGSLEY PUBLISHERS

KINGSLEY BOOKS SERVICES (UK) LTD.

SUITE 28, GREEN STREET ME7 5TJ

GILLINGHAM

Email: kingsleynonye@yahoo.com

Tel/Mobile: +447428153845

Dedication

This book is dedicated to my late father Manfred Gwunireama (Snr), who by his personal achievement taught us the secrets of personal success. His unmitigated love for education drove him through determined struggles and personal sacrifice to achieve a good standard education and became a teacher and a beacon of light in my community in the days when such dreams and achievements were mere contemplations. His legacy has continued to be an inspiration and the catalyst for a massive movement for self-improvement through formal education in the community and beyond.

Acknowledgements

I would like to start by thanking the Almighty God for being my guiding light all through my life's journey thus far. I believe that all my life experiences, challenges and successes have been worth it, as they have all contributed to the person that I am today.

I would like to thank Mr Andy Harrington, the founder of the Public Speakers University (PSU) for his massive impact on my life. The idea of this book was conceived during the 4-day, intensive, public-speaking, training workshop. In fact, the structure of this book is based on the Unique Branded Solution (UBS), which I developed while taking that course. This training helped me re-invent myself and rediscover what is possible for me.

My appreciation also goes to Tony and Nikki Vee of Master Coach, an awesome couple, and to all members of the Professional Speakers Academy. I especially extend my appreciation to my ACE mentor - the one and only Deena Patni. You have all been a great source of inspiration to me.

To all my family, I say a big thank you for your love and belief in me. My wife, Thelma, my son, Goodnews, and my two lovely girls, Precious and Michelle, have been a major source of inspiration while writing this book.

My gratitude goes to my mother, Mrs Deborah Timothy, for her unflinching love, care and prayers. You have always made me feel special. And to my late father, Mr Manfred Gwunireama (Snr) who, through sheer determination and personal struggle, became a beacon of light, laying the foundation of education in my community.

To my uncle, HRM Chief Harry J Etetor, the paramount ruler of the Eastern Obolo Local Government Area, I owe much gratitude. You have always believed in me and provided the much-needed encouragement to succeed. Without this unconditional support, my education would have remained but a dream.

A special thank you to all those who have inspired me through their personal development work, books and videos - Napoleon Hill, Les Brown, Jim Rohn, Tony Robbins, Bob Proctor, Vic Johnson,

Brian Tracy, Darren Hardy, Rhonda Byrne - to mention but a few.

To my friends and colleagues - Pastor Sam, Kingsley Onyekwulije, Grace Charles, Aisha Adegbola, Betty Nsamba, Michelle Chandler, Duke Ellis, Innocent Odu, Gbenga Asigo, Charlotte Jeremy-Cuff, Shedrack Edo - and many others too numerous to mention here, I would like to say thank you for your friendship and encouragement, especially during challenging times.

I would also like to say thank you to all my brothers - Rowland, Smith, Ishmael, Israel, Ezekiel and Timothy - as well as my sisters - Cecilia, Love and Cinderella. The same goes for all my nieces, nephews and cousins. Thank you all for being there for me always.

And, finally, to all those who have encouraged, supported and inspired me on my life's journey, either directly or indirectly - it has not been possible to mention your names individually here, but rest assured that I am eternally grateful to you all.

Table of Contents

Introduction

DISGUST: THE CATALYST OF SUCCESS

"If one advances confidently in the directions of his dreams, and endeavours to live the life which he has imagined, he will meet with success unexpected in common hours." – Henry David Thoreau

The journey to change can be remarkably interesting, challenging and somewhat complicated. We all have personal stories of our life experiences and most of the time, it is more exciting to tell your story from the peak of the mountain that has taken you so much sweat and labour to surmount. Then, the story has great potential to appeal to your audience and become a source of inspiration to them.

But bear in mind that not every experience can be captured perfectly or precisely through verbal or written expression. There is always the possibility that the storyteller will either exaggerate or minimise their experiences. Even so, the most important thing is getting the story out there.

Only then does it have a chance of impacting the life of someone who might draw inspiration from it to change their own circumstances and turn things around. Even if only one person finds my story and this book inspiring, I will have achieved my goal for writing it, making it a worthwhile venture for me.

In this book you will learn how to:

- activate your desire
- resolve to achieve by making a definite decision
- identify your limiting beliefs, challenge, and debunk them
- replace your limiting beliefs with helpful positive beliefs and attitudes
- set goals
- take action to achieve your goals
- measure and review your outcomes
- innovate, re-strategize, and grow

In November 2005, I arrived in the United Kingdom to join my then wife. I had left everything to start a new life. The excitement was great, and the expectations were high; the prospect of making a good life was amazing. Some of you who are immigrants to the West will certainly identify with this feeling. You can only imagine how shattered I was when it turned out that for the first six months, I couldn't get a job despite persistent efforts. I was dead broke and relying on hand-outs from friends and church members. Tension ran high in the home. My wife was becoming very intolerant of my jobless status. Confrontations were common and strong emotions were easily expressed.

Then, in September 2008, we had our first child. I was at that time working as a carer (a Care Support Worker) but my earnings were not enough to support the family in the way I needed to. So, I took a second job just to make my income go a little further. Most days, I would go from one job to the other. My days off were also committed to my second job but the harder I worked, the more difficult it was to meet my financial obligations. Perhaps the most difficult challenge was that my relationship was very unstable and had reached a crisis point. You could imagine what 'Hell' it was that I was swimming in.

My frustration peaked at this time and I was becoming increasingly miserable and fed-up with the situation and life in general. It was very worrying as life was characterised by desperation and mixed, intense emotions. It was a fiasco and I knew that something had to change but wasn't sure what. I was easily lost in my thoughts which were mostly negative and gradually drawn into a depressive state, the harder I pondered the disaster that was facing me. The outlook was very bleak indeed and many questions arose in my overwhelmed mind and I was drained by the continuous stream of negative thoughts - "What else can I do? How do I get ahead? Am I ever going to survive this? What if this …What if that...?".

It was at this point that I was re-introduced to an immensely powerful book, 'Think and Grow Rich' by Napoleon Hill and my life changed dramatically. I knew about this book years before but had not taken the time to read it. This time it was different. I was desperate and hungry for change and I was willing to do anything to get me out of the pit of Hell that I had found myself in. So, I went to work and read and read and made notes as I read. I started following the instructions in the book - writing down my desires and goals and diligently working through the exercises. I poured my heart and soul into it as, after all I had nothing to lose but everything to gain. I remembered the saying 'He that is down needs to fear no fall'. Where could I possibly fall to when I was already flat on the ground?

Reading this book was my light-bulb moment. I started feeling a renewed sense of hope and my self-confidence was gradually being restored. Although the situation had not changed literally speaking, I felt like I had already overcome it. I could see the possibility of change. It was simply the dawn of a new era for me and this kicked-started my personal development journey.

Since then, I have been advancing relentlessly and confidently towards my dream. I have read many other books on personal development, listened to numerous audio programmes on CDs, DVDs, MP3 downloads and even subscribed to Success magazine. I have attended several seminars/workshops and webinars including those by well-known names like Tony Robbins. In fact, I have always been obsessed with personal development and can never have enough of it. The more I get, the hungrier I am for more. I signed up for a few online programmes that would take me a step closer to my goals. Some of these courses turned out to be useless but I always found one or two things to take with me that made it worth the time and money and which added to my knowledge base.

My car is constantly buzzing with personal development talks. When I'm in the shower, my phone is playing personal development stuff like Success Talks, seminars by Tony Robbins or Les Brown on YouTube. When I'm cooking, or walking anywhere, I have my earphones on listening to these seminars. I have stopped listening to news except on the odd occasions when I find myself in a room in which there is news displayed. You see, my view is that I am a late-starter and I'm trying to fill in for all the missing years. I really wish that I had started much earlier but I also believe that it's never too late to start a positive journey. Better late than never, as they say. I must feed my mind to debunk all the negative, limiting beliefs that have taken root for so many years. The investment cost in terms of time and money is high but it is well worth it. I am already getting good dividends from my investment with much more to come. I exude much more self-assurance and when I talk to people, they listen to me. People very easily commend my self-confidence and optimistic outlook, even in the face of challenges.

> **"Whenever you see a successful person you only see the public glories, never the private sacrifices to reach them." — Vaibhav Shah**

The principles I have learnt, and which have helped me on my journey so far, are what I have put together in this book, 'Discover The Super Achiever Within You' to help others who need some encouragement. I hope to help people start believing what is possible for them and find inspiration to press on in life, in spite of where they are now and what challenges they are currently facing. Like guardian angels, these principles have given me guidance in the darkest times and shone their light to illuminate my path and understanding. They have been my reference points and I have found myself going back to them for direction and inspiration. They have helped me get understanding and clarity about my dreams and climb higher on the ladder to the place of attaining success, happiness and fulfilment. These are the ultimate achievements in life. What gain is there if we have everything without happiness and a sense of fulfilment?

I created the D.R.E.A.M.E.R.S SUCCESS PLATFORM from these core principles. This is a programme designed to provide a systematic framework for teaching and coaching people about these success principles. Each one is a step that will guide and instruct you. They operate according to divine laws like the law of gravity, which do not change. They are always available and will work for anyone who dares to employ their services - irrespective of race, religion, abilities or disabilities, educational background, and class. However, for you to have the full benefits of these principles you must run with them, put them to the test by applying them, consistently and persistently, in every area of your life that you want to see changes. These could be in the realms of your physical health, losing weight, for example, or emotional or psychological, financial, spiritual, business or career areas.

We will be following the framework of The D.R.E.A.M.E.R.S SUCCESS PATFORM in this book. So let's get started.

THE D.R.E.A.M.E.R.S SUCCESS PLATFORM

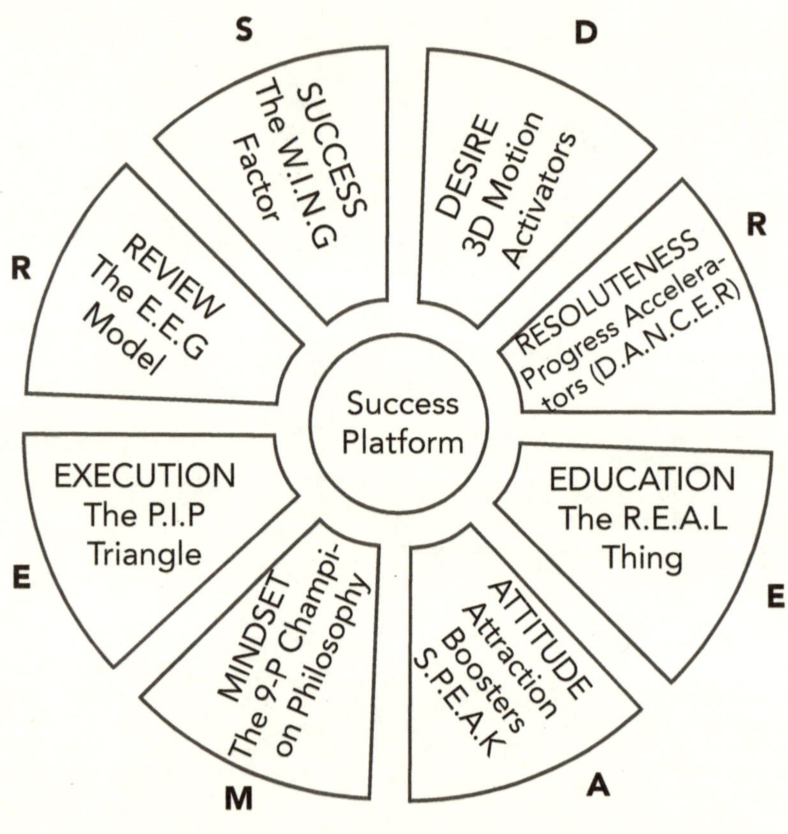

Chapter One

DESIRE – 3D Motion Activators

Desire is the foundation for all achievements. The motion activators are Dreams, Drive and Determination. These build the momentum necessary for turning desire into achievement.

> **"A burning desire to be, and to do is the starting point from which the dreamer must take off." – Napoleon Hill**

We all have desired something in our lives at one point or another. So, the concept of desire is familiar to everyone, including children. What is desire? Desire is a strong feeling of wanting something; it is a strong sense of longing. It is an emotional state of mind that is the foundation of all human achievements. Have you ever achieved something in your life, great or small? Everyone has? How did you get to achieve it? What drove you?

How can desire be stimulated?

Desire is stimulated by human needs and aspirations. For example, hunger creates the desire for food, just as cold creates the desire for heat or protection using clothing. The desire to accomplish something worthwhile in life is what drives men and women to high achievement. For you to obtain great achievement, your desire must be greater than a mere wish. Your desires must have some element of obsession to be able to drive you. This is what differentiates achievers from non-achievers. Humans are driven by their desires. What are your needs? What are your desires? Human needs can be classified into the following categories: financial, emotional, spiritual, business, physical and relationships (personal and business). Maybe you desire breakthrough in one or more areas. Put your desire to work with a sense of obsession. Remember that you have absolute control over your own emotions and can induce your state to suit what you want.

"All human activity is prompted by desire." – Bertrand Russell

Desire in itself is neither positive nor negative. It is a human emotion. But the ways by which humans go about fulfilling their desires can be positive or negative. For instance, you can work to earn money to buy food; or you can choose to go and steal to satisfy your hunger. The beastly act of rape is driven by uncontrollable desire for sex. Greed, too, is a negative way of achieving our desire. We must learn to tame our desires and express them in ways that do not encroach on the rights of other people. Your controlling desire determines your focus, actions, and level of achievement in life.

"You will become as small as your controlling desire; as great as your dominant aspiration." – James Allen

Most advertisements on radio, television, newspapers, magazines, billboards, the internet, and social media, are there to stimulate our desire by painting a picture in our minds to create a longing for those goods or services being advertised. Can you think of any such adverts and how you reacted or responded to them?

In religious circles, a strong desire, along with a sense of obsession, is sometimes misconstrued as having a negative connotation - especially the desire for money and other material things. I strongly disagree with this position. I believe that without desire, nothing good can be created. It is the way in which we pursue our desires that could be negative - such as when we seek to satisfy our desire to the detriment of others. When a desire becomes a dream, man can create the means of achieving it through the power of imagination if there is currently no existing way of doing it. This implies that desire can become a creative force for invention as it can inspire creative imagination and drive.

Dreams

"The size of your success is measured by the strength of your desire; the size of your dream; and how you handle disappointment along the way." — Robert Kiyosaki

Dreams are the mental pictures of our desires created in our minds. What are your dreams or ambitions in life? What are your aspirations? Where do you see yourself in five or ten years from now? Dreams create hope and hope develops faith and faith fuels achievement. Faith is that state of mind where we can achieve the impossible. It is true that the size of our dreams is directly proportionate to the size of our achievements. The size of our achievements is determined by the size of problems we are willing to solve.

As a child, I used to dream big dreams. I would tell my mother, "Mamma when I grow up, I want to be a rich man.... I want to build us a castle (I used to build my castles in the sand) .... I want to feed the poor people..." However, as I grew up, my dreams gradually vanished as I joined the bandwagon of the 'realists' around me. "Be realistic", they would say. "How are you going to achieve these things, are you going to be an armed robber?" I started to become more realistic and logical as dictated by my upbringing and environment. I began to allow the reality of my poor and humble background to steal my dreams. I learnt in church that, 'The love of money is the root of all evil,' and that seeking material wealth was a sin. The rich folks in my community were derided and called names such as evil, greedy, selfish, witches and arrogant. These were the false beliefs about riches that surrounded me and I did not want to bear those tags. There was so much poverty and hunger in the community and to worsen the situation, we took pride in blissful ignorance and stupid and pitiable contentment driven by laziness and lack of aspiration. It was so ingrained in our DNA that it would have been absurd to dream to be different. No-one seemed to dare to be different and dream big dreams. We lived in a culture of small thinking, living in a small world but surrounded by abundance. We worshiped small gods, lived in small huts, had small farms and canoes, married many small wives, had many small children who were not expected to do better than their parents, and died small deaths. Dreaming big or aspiring for riches was considered greedy, selfish and evil. So, everyone was held captive by the chains of these limiting beliefs. Little wonder there was barely progress in the community. We were living testimonies of the biblical declaration, 'As a man thinks in his heart so is he.'

"If you accept a limiting belief, then it will become a truth for you." — Louise Hay

I have big dreams now. It has taken me several years to overcome those limiting beliefs and re-invent myself. How big is your dream? Some people have dreams and goals, but their goals are not big enough to drive them. If I were to ask you where you see yourself in five or ten years' time, what would your response be? For most people, their dream is to wake up every morning and force themselves to go to the work they don't like and earn 'enough' money to pay the bills and put food on their table, riding on the treadmill of life. They pretend they do not want more but inside they know that they want more or at least could do with more. For such people, the only way they get a pay rise is to wait for one. How often does this pay rise come and how much is it? Your guess is as good as mine. You can have more if your dream is big enough. This is absolutely within your control and the power to manifest your dreams lies within you. Yes! Inside of you is where the power lies.

"Shoot for the moon. Even if you miss, you'll land among the stars." - Norman Vincent Peale

After several years of limiting myself, I have finally overcome that culture of dreaming small. And so can you. Yes you, the one reading this right now. You are enough all by yourself to ignite the flame of success that has been lying dormant within you. I believe that I have the potential to do more than I can ever imagine and I expect to realise my dreams. It does not matter what people say about me. My friends have told me, "Manfred you have to be realistic. You are too ambitious." My reply to them is that I am a late-starter and need to try and recover some of the lost years. When I decided to be a public speaker, they questioned my skills and talent. "How will you breakthrough in that industry in the UK?" they asked. "You have an accent and you talk too slowly, no-one will listen to you," they quipped. But I am determined to make it. I believe I have a message of encouragement and inspiration to share with humanity and I will not let my accent hold me back. It is possible! I am prepared to fail my way to success. I am prepared to learn the hard way and I will succeed.

Drive

"The worst bankrupt in the world is the man who has lost his enthusiasm" – H. W. Arnold

Drive refers to the quality of being highly-motivated or enthusiastic about your dreams. Drive fuels the dreams and makes them a powerful force. Without drive, your dream is only a daydream and lacks the power to transform your life. Drive is energy. It is physical and mental energy. Drive is the go-factor. Many people want to improve their lives but lack the drive or motivation to get up and do that which is necessary. A person who is driven is motivated and optimistic, full of energy and enthusiasm. Are you driven? Are you enthusiastic? Most people are not driven because they have not experienced enough pain in their current circumstance. Humans are driven to action by the desire to either move away from pain or move towards pleasure.

I know a family friend who was obese. Although she knew why she was obese (eating too much food with little physical activity) and what she should be doing to help herself, she did nothing. She kept eating more and more without exercise. She hated going for a walk. All she wanted to do was sit in front of the television all day. There was no motivation at all. She always wanted to do it tomorrow but her tomorrow never came until the pain of not changing became too much to bear.

> **"Show me a man who is thoroughly satisfied, and I will show you a failure" – Thomas A Edison**

One day, she suffered a heart attack and nearly died. The doctors warned her about her weight and that she would die if she had another heart attack. This was the wake-up call for her and finally she decided to do something about it. The pain of being an accident waiting to happen and the thought of what would happen to her if she encountered another heart attack, propelled her into action. Have you ever found yourself in a similar situation? Perhaps you know somebody like that. If you did act, how did you find the drive?

This person joined the gym, got an instructor and has been attending regularly ever since. Also, she is now following a weight-loss diet plan. The question is why did she have to wait for a pronouncement from a doctor before acting? I believe that she has always known the root of her problems and what to do to take control but didn't. Drive can be triggered by pain that we want to avoid or a sense of pleasure that is greater than the pain. What is driving you? Do you know that you can deliberately escalate your pain so that it will propel you into action? Or why not put some fire on your desire and let it burn and drive you to your destination just like when we fire the engine of a car to move faster?

Determination

"A man can fail many times, but he isn't a failure until he begins to blame somebody else." – John Burroughs

Determination is the ability to continue towards your goals despite all the obstacles and challenges. The journey to greatness is not a smooth one - it is full of hills and valleys, straight paths and sharp corners, even blind spots.

There is no way of you knowing fully what will happen on the way to achieving your dreams. The man who is determined starts his journey anyway, hoping for the best outcome and prepared for the worst. Waiting for perfect conditions before you begin leads to procrastination which is one of the main killers of dreams.

> **"He who fears being conquered is sure of defeat." – Napoleon Bonaparte**

I remember when I wanted to apply to university. We did not have any money; my father had died and I was living with my mother. But I was so determined, that I started working towards university education not knowing how it would happen. I enrolled for JAMB (Joint Admissions and Matriculation Board) exams with money I borrowed from my uncle. At the time, I was living in my village and working as a peasant fisherman after my secondary education finished. And when I was finally given provisional admission, I used the little savings that I had as a deposit to enrol at the university without knowing where the money for my tuition and upkeep would come from.

In those days we did not have student loans in Nigeria where I come from, so secondary and higher education is mainly financed by your family, your savings or a scholarship, if you are lucky to have one. And do you know what happened? I completed my studies and graduated with a 2:1 degree. It was a journey of faith and it was worth it. I will not bore you with the story of personal sacrifices such as skipping meals, and so forth, but it ended on a good note and that is what is most important. If I had waited for perfect conditions, of-course, I would still be in my village like most of my friends, still working as a fisherman. Therefore, I believe in jumping right in and then sinking or swimming.

The same situation occurred when I wanted to train as a nurse in the United Kingdom. I resigned from my job as a care support worker to study full-time. My colleagues thought I was crazy as I had my family to look after. They suggested I did the course part-time and I argued that that was going to take me longer. I did do it full-time and it did not make much difference to the living conditions of my family. I'm not suggesting that this would necessarily be the best option for everyone else, but if you want something badly enough, you will find the way to achieve it. It might not make much difference to your situation, but you will be the better for it. Fear of the unknown holds people back. Do not let this be you. Take the first step and the second .... one step at a time and it will work out. Don't always wait to have all the resources or support before you begin. It is called FAITH.

So what am I on about? What I am saying is that if you have a burning desire for anything, resolve within yourself to get it and just start from where you are and with what you have. Start small if you must. Don't delay starting because you haven't got much. I believe that there is grace in motion; start doing something towards that dream NOW. It may be just a phone call to someone who can guide you. But remember that it is not going to be a smooth ride. There will be obstacles on your way. However, they are not there to stop you but to make you stronger by building your character. This is true. Be determined and keep going. What you will discover is that you will become a better person even if you did not quite reach the original goal you set out to achieve. Also, be prepared to adjust your goals along the way if necessary.

We have seen that desire is the very foundation of any achievement. And that Dreams, Drive and Determination are essential to propel our desire into motion. In the next chapter we are going to look at how to build momentum and make progress towards achieving our dreams.

Chapter Two

RESOLUTENESS – Progress Accelerators (The D.A.N.C.E.R)

"Every human mind is a great slumbering power until awakened by a keen desire and by definite resolution to do." – Edgar F Roberts

The man who has resolved will either find a way or make one. The strength of your resolution is determined by a definite decision and what you focus on. Every New Year, we hear people make new-year resolutions. You are probably familiar with empty resolutions. They go something like: *I'm going to lose weight; I'm going to quit smoking; I'm going to get a new job; I'm going to learn how to play an instrument this year.* These are not resolutions. These are mere wishes until they are backed by strong decisions and focus. It is not surprising most new-year resolutions never get to February before they're given up - if people manage to start something at all. Changing your life requires more than just wishing to do something – it takes real action to make it happen.

Why do people make lasting resolutions? The F. I. N. D. E. R factor

How do we come to make strong and lasting resolutions? Why do people make resolutions and not follow them through? These are some of the questions that come to mind when we see ourselves or others making and following through with their resolutions while others do not. The fact is that genuine resolve is triggered by any of the following factors, which I call the **F.I.N.D.E.R** factor.

F- Fear of failure, or of losing control or losing something special. If someone were to put a gun to your head and asked you to do something, how would you feel? Do you think you would be more likely to do it? Why? The fear of losing your life if you did not. The fear of losing a loved one for example, or a job or a business or experiencing a breakup in a relationship has the potential to drive us to make changes and sustain them. The fear of falling behind on your bills might force you to take action like going out to do a job you do not like.

I – Insight – Coming to a new realisation or revelation intuitively. This could be because of new knowledge or understanding and could happen while reading, listening to something or meditating. New realisation can drive us to work towards our goals in life in a sustainable way.

N- Near-miss or a life-changing event – for example, having a heart attack because of obesity. I once worked with a patient who told me how he managed to turn over a new leaf and transformed his life following a very traumatic experience. He was part of a group of friends who led a lifestyle of alcohol and drugs and always living under the influence of those substances. One day, they went to a party and were all drunk. On their way home from the party, they had a ghastly motor accident and some of his friends died. He was lucky to survive but still suffers from the trauma of the event. And since then, he has vowed to himself to never again touch alcohol and recreational drugs and he has stuck to this. Good for him, don't you think? Extreme but a true experience. For some of us it takes an extremely painful memory for us to make the changes necessary to transform our lives.

D – Disgust – When we get to the point that we say to ourselves: *I've had it.* This might be following a humiliation or an embarrassment. I shared earlier the story of how the humiliation of falling behind on my bills brought so much anger and frustration to my life. And at one point, I said to myself that my situation MUST change. And it did. Have you ever been in such a situation where you just could not let it continue the way it was? How did you feel? What did you do? For most people, that is when they act. That is when they decide to move on from a relationship that has been toxic or abusive for so long.

E – Ego – A desire to protect our sense of pride and superiority could lead us to make a lasting resolution so as not to be seen as a coward. Ego might not necessarily mean pomposity. This is one reason public declaration works because once everyone knows that this is what you said you wanted to do, they will hold you accountable.

And chances are that you might not want to lose face and this could be your driving force to act. Remember the power of peer pressure but this time in a positive way.

R – Reason – We need to have a strong enough reason to be motivated to make sustainable changes in our lives. We are all wired to respond to pain and pleasure in one form or another. If the perceived benefits of the change are much more than the potential pains, we are more likely to be motivated to follow through with our resolutions. Also, ask yourself why you need to be successful? Maybe as a parent, you want to protect your children from hardship or give them the best chances in life. When driven by an extraordinarily strong reason, you will not make excuses, neither will you consider the weather nor obstacles when taking necessary action towards your goals. What are your reasons? Why is it important that you lose weight or succeed in life? Only you can answer this question.

> **"If you really want to do something, you'll find a way. If you don't, you'll find an excuse" – Jim Rohn**

Progress Accelerators (The D.A.N.C.E.R)

Now let us examine our Progress Accelerators. These are key elements to a lasting resolution that are sustainable and that produce the desired results. The components of the progress accelerators are made up in the acronym D.A.N.C.E.R - which stands for - Decide, Act, Nourish, Concentrate, Evaluate and Repeat. I believe that you cannot DANCE without movement, as all forms of dancing involve one form of motion or another. Now let us examine each in more detail -

D – Decide The most important ingredient to a lasting resolution is definite decision. Decision is particularly important because it is an indication of how serious the resolution is and a willingness to do what it takes.

> **"There is no more miserable human being than one in whom nothing is habitual but indecision." – William James**

We are all products of our decisions. We are where we are today because of the decisions we made yesterday and the decisions we make today will determine where we are going to be tomorrow. The change we desire in our lives can only be made possible by a decision. My migration to the United Kingdom to join my then 'sweetheart' was because of a decision. I clearly had other options. If I had decided otherwise, my life would certainly have taken a different turn. Perhaps I could have had a successful political career, as I was very much involved in politics in my community and state. It was a difficult and emotional decision but I was prepared to sacrifice the perceived potential benefits of deciding otherwise.

Remember 'opportunity cost' in economic theory - the cost of the forgone alternative. My apologies if you did not study economics and this is a strange concept. Please look it up! The idea is that every time we decide, we are forgoing the potential benefits and setbacks of alternative decisions. Therefore, we should not take our decisions lightly. Get into the habit of analysing your decisions by identifying the pros and cons of each before taking a stand. If you do this with small, everyday decisions it becomes easier when making the big decisions in life, such as choosing a life partner or a career.

When I was working as a nurse in a mental health rehabilitation unit, I became fed-up with all the things that were going on there. Nothing personal against any of my colleagues and managers. In fact, they were very lovely people and I enjoyed working with them. Some of them are still my best friends now. However, the administrative bottlenecks were ridiculous and this is common in most jobs when you are an employee. I am sure you can relate to this. We could not even decide when to take our holidays in the unit. We had to make a request and it was up to the manager to decide whether we could have the days requested or not. We could not decide what shifts we wanted to work, we just followed whatever was rostered for us. Basically, we had to plan our lives around our work rotas!

I considered this a complete loss of control; I felt that my life was being controlled by someone else. My colleagues would whine and moan but did nothing. For many years, I did too until I decided that I was going to resign from my permanent post and work flexibly through an agency. This gave me the flexibility to work when I wanted to and a sense of being more in control. I earned more money working this way and could choose when to work, which I found very liberating, at least in the short term. Later, I was fed-up with having to work too many hours and not earning any money when I did not go to work, so I took a permanent job again but one that allowed me more flexibility. However, this was after I had managed to set up my own business which was running with minimal input from me. As part of my personal development training, I learnt that profit was better than wages so I started working on ways to build passive income whereby I could still be making money while I was sleeping. How nice?! However, this is a topic for another time…

Where are you right now? What decisions did you make in the past that have brought you to this point? Where do you want to be in five or ten years' time? You can create it with a decision or a series of decisions right now. Remember that *not* deciding is also a decision. Indecision simply means that you are saying, "I don't really care where I am in ten years' time - let external conditions determine this for me." I hope that you do not leave your destiny to chance when you have all the power to determine it by just making a definite decision. You have the power to determine your destiny - just make the decision. Do not worry about how you are going to achieve it, that will work out itself. Do not wait to see the whole staircase, just start with the first step and you will see the next, and the next, and the next…….

> **"True decisions are the catalysts for turning our dreams into reality" – Anthony Robbins**

I have decided that in five or ten years' time, I want to reach out and make a difference in people's lives by sharing my knowledge and experience with them and opening their eyes to the possibilities that life holds for them. I want to inspire them to aspire to greater things in their lives. I have worked as a clinician in different clinical settings as a mental health practitioner and have seen the despair in people's lives, their whining and moaning, their complaining about their jobs, relationships, and so on. Yet, they still feel unable to take control of these situations, unable to decide to do something about them. I have also seen the devastation bad or wrong decisions have caused in the lives of some of my patients. For example, those who are addicted to substances like alcohol and recreational drugs and the helplessness of their positions as they struggle to take back control of their lives with extraordinarily little or no success. I have seen first-hand, lives shattered beyond repair, relationships destroyed, noble careers end in tatters.

"It does not take much strength to do things, but it requires great strength to decide on what to do" – Elbert Hubbard

What could prevent us from deciding for change?

FEAR is probably the main factor. It was for me for a long time. What are you afraid of? Mine was the fear of failure. What would people think of me? What would they say if I failed? Or is it fear of success? What if I succeed and cannot handle it? You see, I did not want to make a fool of myself by trying something and failing to achieve what I set out to do. I allowed this to deter me for a long time. I remember before I attended the Public Speakers University, I doubted myself as a speaker. I said I did not have the 'British accent' so I would not be accepted as a speaker in the

United Kingdom. But somehow, I managed to overcome this fear by reassuring myself that if I have a great message or a story, people will listen to me. I then proceeded to attend the speakers university, anyway, to acquire some presentation skills and gain some self-confidence. I said to myself that I would give it a shot and I did. My confidence grew when I heard the testimonies of other speakers and I said to myself, "Manfred, you can do this!" Sometimes all we require is a little polishing and dusting of our skills. You can do anything you set your mind on. It is possible!

"Many a man never fails because he never tries" – Norman MacEwan

So, what is holding you back? What is it that you think you have not got? Look! Do not let anything stop you from going after your dreams. Just take the plunge! You will be surprised what you discover about yourself. The safety of your comfort zone is not where you will grow. The tortoise only makes progress when it sticks out its neck from its shell. It is not going to be easy but if you are persistent, you will achieve your dreams. Do not leave the key decisions of your life to someone else because if you don't make those decisions, someone else will make them for you somehow, directly or indirectly.

A – Action is another important aspect of a lasting resolution. Taking a step further from your decision and making the effort is what is required to produce the expected result. Without action on our part, the resolution is dead. We need to take massive, sustained action to get what we want. This is where most people fail. It is sometimes easier to decide to do something than to find the courage to act on your decision. Fear plays a big role here, too, also lack of self-confidence or an inferiority complex. There's the fear of failure or rejection or fear of what could happen. What is your own fear? The solution to this kind of fear is to face it anyway. Think of what the worst-case scenario could possibly be if you took the action. It is probably not death! If you are asking for a favour, the worst case is perhaps somebody saying, 'No' to you. But what if they say 'Yes'? How would you know if you did not try? Most of the time, when we summon the courage to attempt something we are afraid of, we realise that the outcome wasn't as bad as we thought it would be. Lack of confidence could be the result of feeling inadequate in the situation; like not having the required qualifications, not having much going for you, your background or lack of experience, and so on. I recommend that you get some help if necessary and just take the plunge and go for what you want. If you do not succeed the first time, review the situation and change your strategy and try again, and again, and again.......

N- Nourish your action to sustain it. How do you nourish your action? By devising a system that works for you and that will encourage you to repeat the action regularly and consistently over a long period of time. This could mean preparing and following a schedule, attending a support group, or getting a coach or mentor. Consistency is essential for getting the desired result, so being able to take productive action on a consistent basis is critical to your success. Start with small steps and build up a daily routine, then increase the action as your routine becomes a part of you. But make sure you stick rigidly with your routine. This requires discipline and sacrifice. Changing your life is not easy but if it is important, then it is worth the price. Small disciplines are important, like waking up earlier than is normal for you in order to do that exercise, or cutting down on your food portions, or saving 10% of your income every month. Maybe you want to read fifteen pages of something inspirational every day. Like little drops of water that can make an ocean, small changes or little disciplines applied consistently over time can make a huge difference in your outcome.

C – Concentration or Focus is another key ingredient of a strong resolution and follows from the decision. Focusing suggests that you know what you want in life. If you do not really know what you want, you need to first identify what you want out of life? Ask yourself this question: 'What do I want my life to be like in five, ten or twenty years from now? What am I passionate about in life? What outcome do I want from my life?' These can be specific to an aspect of your life. If you are not focused, it is amazingly easy to be distracted even when you appear to be making good progress or have obtained good success. Sometimes distraction is very subtle, such as being praised when you are doing well.

This might not look like distraction but is known to have caused many great men and women to derail. My suggestion is to give little attention to both praise and criticism because these hold great potential to distract you. It takes a lot of time and energy to answer all your critics or those who praise you. Always remember that you cannot please everyone - whatever you do, you will attract critics and fans and both can be equally good and bad influences and if you give them too much attention, you are likely to derail. Learn to use them for your greater good. Remember that in the game of football, like in many other sports, what ultimately counts are the final scores, not the amount of cheers or boos. And it is not over until it is over. So, start and keep going.

When you are driving a car, you must concentrate on the task and on where the road leads and not be distracted otherwise you will crash. If you are a driver, you will agree that once you are behind the wheel there are a thousand-and-one things that beg for your attention including phone calls, text messages, pretty ladies or handsome men on the sidewalk, fancy cars driving past that must be seen, and so on. It takes discipline to remain focused and maintain your concentration on the task and your destination. You must bear this in mind!

Also remember that you do not need to see the full length of the road before you start off. And usually, at every corner you take, you can only see a small stretch of the road. The same applies to our dreams. Once you have made a definite decision about what you want for your life, you need to stay focused on this if your goals are to be attained.

> **"You don't need to see the whole staircase. Just take the first step." – Martin Luther King Jr**

Focus on the result or your expected outcome, bearing in mind that there may be a need for diversion. This implies that you may need to change your approach or strategy. This is an important aspect of creating change. As noted above, I can assure you that there will be many distractions on the way, some very subtle and appealing. I remember when I resigned from my job as a nurse in a psychiatric hospital. My manager called me and asked me what they could do to make me stay and even assured me of a pay rise. Suddenly, I realised that I was a valued member of the team.

Another time, when I wanted to start my own business, I called a friend who was already established in the same line of work to ask for guidance. He invited me to his house and after some conversations about how ready I was, he warned me that it was not as easy as I thought and reminded me that I did not have any experience in that field. He then asked me to join him in *his* business and be responsible for developing it in another district. This was very tempting as I thought to myself, "This is a good idea, Manfred. It is a fantastic opportunity to gain some experience." But thank goodness that the arrangement didn't work out and I was able to refocus on setting up my own business which was my original desire.

Sometimes, distractions come in very subtle ways totally disguised as opportunities. And it could take you months or even years to realise that it only served to distract you from your original goal. So, watch out for these subtle signs and never sacrifice your dreams for anything, except what is essential in helping you to pursue your goals. But be mindful! When you have clarity about your goals in life, you might find that, sometimes, it is better to wait at the bottom of the stairs you want to climb, rather than be at the top of the ladder you don't want.

Evaluate your journey and the destination. You need to undertake a regular review of your results to see if you are hitting your target or not. This is a time to reflect or ponder on the journey so far. Life's journey is not always straightforward. Having time to evaluate will reassure you that you are still on track or that you need to make some adjustments to your plan, strategy and even your goal to enable you achieve your desired objectives. Be flexible and willing to make changes where necessary. Determine what is working well and what is not, consider alternative strategies like embracing new technologies that could enhance your efforts and help you to reach your goals quicker. I have covered this in more details in chapter 6.

Repeat the whole process. Go back to action, nourish, concentrate, and evaluate

Chapter Three

EDUCATION - The R.E.A.L Thing

"The men who succeed are the efficient few. They are the few who have the ambition and will power to develop themselves" – Herbert N. Casson

Education is a particularly important factor in the achievement of our goals in life. But what is education? Is it going to school? Education is more than just going to school to learn. It is the acquisition of knowledge. This could be skills, values and beliefs and learning these could happen in a formal or informal setting. Methods of learning could occur through teaching, training, research, discussions, and storytelling. Knowledge is an enormously powerful tool in the hands of the people who care enough to apply it. It is, however, not extremely useful if it is not applied or put to work. Ignorance is not an option if you genuinely want to succeed. It is a cankerworm that eats deep into the fabric of the lives of so many. Learning brings growth and progress.

> **"Ignorance is a voluntary misfortune"– Nicholas Ling**

I don't believe that there is much difference between the ignorant person and the person who has knowledge but doesn't use it. Knowledge is like money; it is not useful except when used in exchange for what we want.

Formal education alone will not take us far. Personal development is invaluable if we must make real impact in our own lives and make a difference in the lives of other people. According to Jim Rohn: *Formal education can give us a job, but self-education can make us a fortune.*

How do we acquire knowledge through personal development? I call this the R.E.A.L Thing. This is an acronym for Read, Engage, Attend and Listen. Now let us examine each in detail.

Read and study Reading and studying are key ways whereby knowledge can be acquired. However, the quality of our lives will reflect the quality of books and materials that we have read and studied.

> **"The man who does not read good books has no advantage over the man who can't read them."- Mark Twain**

Positive and inspirational books are key tools in re-inventing us and could inspire us to make a fortune. It takes self-discipline to engage in productive learning and only ambitious and enterprising people take their learning seriously whether as a student, civil servant, a man in uniform, a self-employed technician or a business executive. Little wonder, then, that most people would rather spend hours watching TV and reading lightweight magazines than reading books and magazines that would have a positive impact on their lives. I hope this is not you.

Feed your mind with positive and inspiration materials and your life will change drastically. When I was having challenges in my finances, it was inspirational books that restored my self-confidence, gave me clarity and helped me begin to see that I could do much better than I was doing. So please be mindful of what you feed your minds because you are a reflection of the books you have read, and you cannot grow beyond your knowledge.

Engage with what you are reading and carry out the exercises and activities. It is important that we apply the knowledge we gain from reading/studying into our lives so that we can enjoy the benefits of possessing such knowledge. Remember, knowledge is only power when you put it to the test. Be open-minded to receive instructions and inspiration from what you are reading. Have you ever bought a gadget and tried to set it up without first consulting the users' manual? I have done this many times and if you are like me, you will also have been stuck many times before finally consulting the manuals, only to learn that you had done it all wrong. Wouldn't it have saved time to consult the instructions first? Sure, it would. But why didn't I do it? Because I assumed I knew better. This is the situation we all find ourselves in sometimes and it is incredibly sad indeed. We end up wasting time, energy and sometimes lose money because we have caused irreparable damage to the gadget before referring to the manual. I suggest you get some knowledge in any area of business you wish to venture into and be mindful to apply the knowledge to get the best outcome.

> **"Things don't turn up in this world until somebody turns them on" – James A Garfield**

Attend live events like seminars and workshops as these are very useful methods of gaining the knowledge and skills that you need to succeed in every aspect of your life – financial, business, spiritual, physical, emotional and in our relationships. So, in addition to reading positive and inspirational books and materials, I recommend that you attend relevant seminars and workshops to further your knowledge and skills and grow beyond your comfort zone. Many people do not attend these because of the cost. This is sad because they don't seem to appreciate that the acquisition of knowledge is an investment which can provide returns significantly above the cost.

Think of who you become from the knowledge you have gained from seminars and workshops. What financial value can you place on that? If you can take a loan to buy a car or other items that give you temporary satisfaction or to pay for tuition to study at university which does not necessarily guarantee you a decent job or a decent life, why can't you treat your personal development in the same way? In my experience, attending seminars and workshops accelerated my growth in ways books could not. It is expensive but it is a worthy investment with potential for great fortune. Just one idea you get from a seminar could change your life completely. It is also an invaluable opportunity for networking. In addition, there is usually a supercharged atmosphere at these events which can provide tremendous inspiration and motivation.

> **"If a man empties his purse into his head, no man can take it away from him. An investment in knowledge pays the best interest." – Benjamin Franklin**

Listen to CDs/DVDs, podcasts and videos on YouTube and other websites at home, in the car, while going for a walk or running. Take full advantage of modern technology and download videos on your mobile devices and take them with you anywhere you go and listen to them. I listen to inspirational videos and downloaded materials in the car, while jogging or walking, while waiting for an appointment or a meeting, and so on. And these have helped influence my mindset for the better. The Bible says that faith comes from hearing and repeated hearing of the Word of God. This does not only apply to spiritual materials but also to watching and listening to positive and inspirational materials over and over until it sinks into our soul and influences how we see and think about events happening around us - call it our 'world view'. We need to be mindful what we listen to. Watching and listening to bad and negative materials will likewise amplify negative reasoning and thoughts which can lead to depression, anger, violence, and avoidable sufferings.

> **"Whenever you see a successful person you only see the public glories, never the private sacrifices to reach them." – Vaibhav Shah**

In addition to your learning, you need to build relationships and a network of support with like-minded people. Get a coach or mentor. Join a community of like-minded persons who can share their knowledge, ideas and experiences with you. You do not want to hang out with negative, want-nothing people who will discourage you and try to pull you down. Remember that your mind is like a garden and requires diligent minding to prosper. If you neglect to make conscious, deliberate effort to remove the weeds and nourish your plants, the garden of your mind will be taken over by the weeds. And they do not need your permission to do this. Remember that by natural law, what you sow is what you will reap. You cannot plant oranges and expect to reap apples. So, if you feed your mind always with violent and negative materials, that is exactly what you will reap but in greater quantity because what we plant has a tendency to multiply.

In this chapter we have reviewed the importance of education as a key element to realising our dreams. We have looked at various ways we can acquire knowledge which includes reading and researching, listening to audio or video materials, attending live events and webinars and actually engaging and applying the knowledge we have gained into our daily lives.

Chapter Four

ATTITUDE (The attraction Boosters - S.P.E.A.K)

"Attitude is everything. The state of your life is nothing more than a reflection of your state of mind." – Wayne Dyer

According to *Dictionary.cambridge.org*, 'attitude' is defined as a feeling or opinion about something or someone, or a way of behaving that is caused by this. Your attitude greatly influences your feeling and behaviour towards that person or thing. Sometimes, you cannot help how you feel about something but you can certainly control how you behave. So, the real question is not how you feel about a situation but what you do with how you feel. How do you react or respond to something especially if you feel strongly about it or do not agree with it? A mature approach demands that you *respond* and not *react* to it. Now, what is the difference between the two? Responding implies a thoughtful and controlled process, while reacting means that you do not give much thought about the impact of your reaction on other people.

Attitude is a decision and it is totally within your control. The fact is that your attitude can influence greatly the outcomes in your life. It has been said that life is 10% what happens to us and 90% how we respond or react to it. A bad attitude is like a flat tyre. Once you have a flat tyre, you cannot make much progress until you have fixed it. And daring to drive around with a flat tyre is risking a crash or damaging the rims. The good news is that bad attitude like flat tyres can be fixed. So, do not risk it, fix it.

"It is your attitude, not your aptitude that determines your altitude." – Zig Ziglar

A positive attitude is critical for success. It helps you control your emotional response to challenges and therefore enables you to make better decisions. A positive attitude will attract good and helpful relationships that can make the difference between success and failure. It will also help you to accept and embrace challenges, take responsibility for your actions, and change more easily. Just a little change in your negative attitude can make a huge difference.

"Attitude is a little thing that makes a big difference." – Winston Churchill

A good and positive attitude has the potential to promote you and attract good things to your life, whether it is in business, relationships, work, school, or the community. On the other hand, a bad and negative attitude has the potential to pull you down. A great relationship, that has taken years to build, could be destroyed by a single bad attitude. It takes one little mistake for all your years of goodness and credibility to be completely ruined and forgotten. This is because people are naturally wired to look for what could go wrong and they find it fascinating. This explains why the bad and negative news makes the biggest headlines. Do not let a bad and negative attitude drown you. Remember, it is all within your control and you can do something about it.

How do we cultivate a great positive attitude? Cultivating a great attitude is a decision you can make. I have come up with the acronym **S. P. E. A. K** to give you some insight into some of the things that you could do to change your attitude. S.P.E.A.K stands for Self-awareness, Purpose, Experience, Association and Knowledge.

Self-awareness: Understanding yourself and how your negative attitude could be adversely impacting yourself and the people around you could help you to be more sensitive to others. Self-awareness is critical in building and maintaining a good relationship with your spouse, your family, business partners, customers, and colleagues. It can help you to know what you are best at, when to ask for help and what and when to refer to someone higher in authority.

Discovering who you really are can be very empowering, especially if you have the courage to face the truth about it and are serious about making yourself a better person. I know of people who appear to know that they behave in certain ways which are negative but are very reluctant to make changes. They say, "That is who I am…I cannot help it". I do not believe that they cannot help it if they really want to. It is only an excuse to continue in their negative behaviours because of the selfish purpose it serves them. Let this not be you. And if you are struggling to understand yourself, ask a trusted friend who will not mince words in telling it to you as it is. But do not take their feedback personally, see it as an opportunity to make changes and become a better you.

Purpose: Living with purpose can have an impact on how we behave. You have to have a strong enough purpose for your dreams. Clarity of purpose enables you to focus on what is important and act deliberately to progress towards achieving your goals in life. Jack Canfield said: *Clarify your purpose. What is the why behind everything you do? When you know this in life or design, it is very empowering, and the path is clear.*

A person who has a clear purpose in life knows when to speak, when to be silent and when to act. They also realise that a great attitude will attract to them the people and resources they need to achieve their goals. On the contrary, people without a purpose behave in very selfish ways as they believe that they have nothing to lose anyway.

Experience: Your personal experience of the negative attitude of others could help you to understand how other people feel about your own negative attitude and how it might be impacting them. In the same vein, your positive experiences should teach you how other people feel when they are treated positively.

I believe that we have all got some experiences of good or bad attitudes. How do you feel about great customer service? How about extremely poor customer service, especially where a member of staff has spoken very rudely to you? I once had an unbelievably bad experience in a local corner shop. The lady behind the counter was very rude and hostile because I had asked about the price of an item. I obviously could not see clearly the price label on the item as it had faded. When I approached her, she replied angrily, "The price is written there. Can't you see?" I was shocked and never went back there. She might have been having a bad day but that cost the shop a valuable customer. And what if other customers had the same experience with her and decided not to use that shop again?

Positive attitude is a skill that can be leaned. Anybody can learn it. How much does it cost to smile at someone? Nothing, I suppose you said. A smile can attract a smile and can brighten the whole day for you. So, make deliberate effort to practice positive attitude. It has the potential to attract excellent people to you and open doors of opportunity for great and empowering relationships.

Association: As the saying goes: *Tell me who your friends are, and I will tell you who you are.* Who do you hang out with? Your attitude will reflect the attitude of your closest allies. Changing your friends and associates could drastically improve your attitude. I once heard Les Brown use this example: *If you go out for a walk with another person, its either you that adjusts to their pace or they adjust to yours.* This is true with attitude. It is also true that you are most likely to be affected by a negative attitude than a positive one. For instance, if most of your friends are smokers or drug users, it is more likely that you will be drawn into their habits than they will quit to be like you.

To develop a positive attitude, you need to re-evaluate your associates, kick out negative people from your life and replace them with people who have a positive attitude. Practice the concept of OQP (Only Quality People) and you will attract people who will lift you up, rather than those who will pull you down. Do not forget that it is possible for you to outgrow a particular group that you currently associate with. One indication of this is when you no longer have anything positive to learn from your group and this might be a good time to move on to a new circle if you want to continue to grow.

Knowledge: Lessons you learn from stories in books, movies, teachings and trainings could help you to have new realisations and therefore change your attitude for the better. Mentoring and coaching can be immensely helpful in identifying those little negative attitudes that sometimes you don't even realise you have but are doing much damage to your image. I believe that attitude is a skill that can be learned or unlearned. Knowledge from personal development activities and events can help you to re-evaluate your attitude and make adjustments where necessary, so that you can attract the people to help you achieve your goals. It has made me a better person. It can help you, too, if you apply it to your life.

Let me emphasise here that knowledge alone is not real power. It is only knowledge *applied* that has the potential to bring about change. You could learn and have knowledge of all the 'secrets' of success but they will amount to nothing if you do not apply this knowledge to daily situations in your life. For example, you could learn and have all the theorical knowledge about how to drive a car but until you get behind the wheel and apply that knowledge to drive a car, your knowledge alone cannot move it. We live in a world of many so-called 'experts', most of whom only have theoretical understanding with extraordinarily little or no practical experience and no track record of applying their knowledge to produce anything. If theorical knowledge alone produced wealth, professors would be the richest people on Earth. Sadly, they are not.

Chapter Five

MINDSET (The 9-P's champion philosophy)

"You are today where your thoughts have brought you; you will be tomorrow where your thoughts will take you." – James Allen

Mindset' is defined on vocabulary.com as, 'a habitual or characteristic mental attitude that determines how you interpret and respond to situations.' The mindset of an individual is determined by their belief systems, culture, background, and life experiences. These eventually enable them to formulate their personal philosophy which influences how they see the world, how they think and how they interpret situations. This then determines how they respond to events happening around them.

These philosophies or paradigms, when fully-rooted and developed, can be difficult to change, as the individual tends to build a protective wall around them. And, in some cases, people are willing to do anything to protect their mindsets as these have formed part of their identity. In extreme cases, people are willing to die for their long-ingrained beliefs and practices.

Some mindsets can be empowering and some limiting. Your mindset has a lot to do with your state in life and whether you succeed or fail because what you believe about yourself and other people, will eventually play out in your life. If for example, you hold the belief that being rich is bad or evil you will detest riches and will never attract it.

Beliefs are incredibly powerful and can make or destroy the whole person. They affect how you cope with challenges because it is your interpretation of conflict and resolution that determines how you respond or react to it. The fact is, situations only carry the meanings that we give to them. Two people could face the same situation and give different interpretations to it. One might be positive and empowering, while the other is negative, based on that person's views or perspectives, history, and belief systems.

A good illustration is the story of six blind men who went to feel an elephant to gain an idea of what it was like. You are probably familiar with this story, whether it is true or not is not the issue here but the lessons it carries.

"Hey, the elephant is like a pillar," said the first man who touched the leg of the elephant.

"Oh, no! It is like a rope," said the second man who touched the tail.

"Oh, no! It is like a thick branch of a tree," said the third man who touched the trunk.

"It is like a big hand fan," said the fourth man who touched the ear.

"It is like a huge wall," said the fifth man who touched the belly.

"It is like a solid pipe," said the sixth man who touched the tusk of the elephant.

So, the six men touching the same elephant, each had a unique impression of what the elephant was, based on their personal experience. This is basically how we, as humans, tend to interpret situations that happen in our lives. And when driven by limiting beliefs, we assume that only our point of view is correct. The man with an empowering mindset, however, seeks more understanding and having acquired further information, has a more complete picture. We can call this 'the big picture' which is more likely to prompt us to interpret the situation in a positive way.

Many people, in the same way, are captives or prisoners of their limiting beliefs or negative mindsets. It is only by changing such mindsets that they can be liberated. The ability to control our mindset is a great gift. There are many things that happen in our lives that we cannot control. But we can control how we interpret and respond to them. Isn't this amazing? Why, then, are we not using this power? This is the power that can change everything about us and lift us from a place of unhappiness, failure, poverty or sickness to the place where our dreams can be realised. A rigid mindset is one of the world's greatest barriers to progress or true and lasting peace - especially when linked with religion. People taking extreme positions based on their ingrained belief systems and mindsets is the foundation of many avoidable conflicts, wars, racism, homophobia and so forth.

> **"Mind is a flexible mirror, adjust it to see a better world." — Amit Ray**

Creating a Positive Mind-Set:

There are several elements that make up a positive and empowering mindset. We are going to look at nine of them in this book. These are what I have tagged *The 9P's Champion Philosophy.*

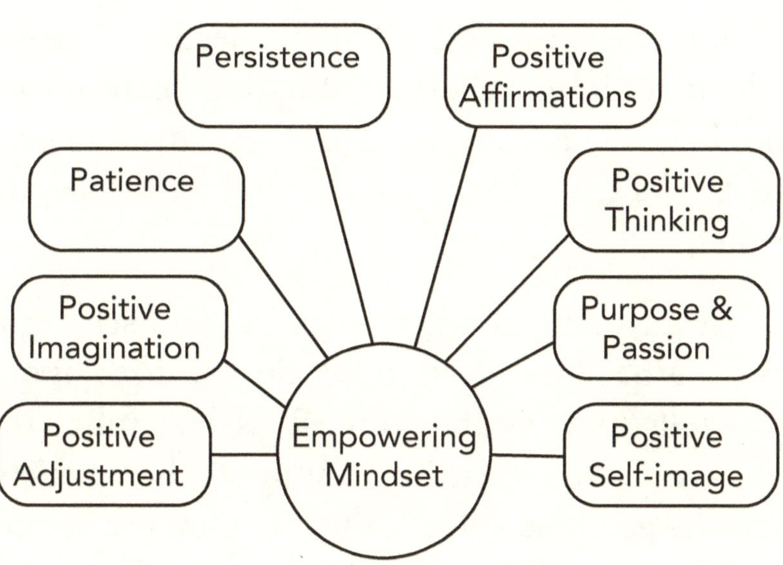

Positive Self-Image:

"They can conquer who believe they can."
– Virgil

Self-confidence is a key ingredient in attaining success and this can only be achieved when you have a positive image of yourself. Without believing in your ability to accomplish something or overcome a challenge, it will be exceedingly difficult for you to reach your goals. We need to believe in ourselves. How can we do this? We need to realise that we are being held captive by our negative or limiting beliefs. We need to identify which limiting beliefs or thinking patterns are holding us back and challenge them. Then, replace them with a positive and more helpful belief.

With an open mind, re-examine yourself right now. What limiting mindset do you have about yourself and your abilities? Re-examine the arguments you are using to support these beliefs. Challenge these ideas. What if they are wrong and based on false premises? Replace them with positive thoughts about yourself and abilities. Say, 'I can' or at least say 'It's possible.' At times, self-doubt will come but keep going and trust that you will make it if you do not give up. Make sure you do not indulge in self-pity no matter what situation you are currently facing. Self-pity is a cankerworm and only leads to one destination - mediocrity.

Purpose and Passion

"He that thinks he can afford to be negligent is not far from being poor." – Samuel Johnson

Do you know what your purpose in life is? Find out why you do what you do. Living without a purpose is like leaving your home and getting on the bus without a destination in mind. Martin Luther King, Jr said, "If a man hasn't discovered something that he will die for, he isn't fit to live." I believe that there is something that we are all meant to accomplish in this life that will contribute to the greater good of humanity. Being purpose-driven helps us to focus on what is important and inspires us to put in whatever it will take to achieve it. Lack of purpose is lack of clarity.

Get clarity before you start otherwise you might well be travelling south when you were meant to be in the north. Just drifting along is not the way to live. I know because I have lived my life just drifting along. When I had the option of demanding more, I would simply say, "anything will do please", only to regret this a moment later when I observed others asking specifically for what they wanted and getting it. Thankfully, I do not do this any more because I know now what I want and do not hesitate to ask for it - and even more - at the slightest opportunity.

What about you? Are you just drifting along and hoping for the best? Or are you demanding what you want from life because you know what it is?

Knowing what you want out of life will help you to set the right goals to achieve it. It will help you to focus and when you are focused, you can see the obstacles and know them for what they are. You will also be in a better position to surmount them because you know what you are looking to achieve, even if it takes you one thousand attempts like the great Thomas Edison. He set his mind to invent the electric bulb and never gave up, even after several attempts. Sports people understand this better because they know how to spend hours, days, weeks, and months trying to perfect just one skill. But we all see them in the spotlight and think it is as easy as they make it seem.

"The worst bankrupt in the world is the man who has lost his enthusiasm – H. W. Arnold

A purposeful life is driven by passion. We will only find ourselves in the zone and performing at the peak of our creativity when we are passionate about our purpose and our passion combines with our talent. Are you passionate about what you do? If your answer is no, then you need to re-invent yourself. You need to find out what you are passionate about and do it. That is where you will have a sense of fulfilment and make the greatest impact. Passion will give you the drive and enthusiasm that will sustain you when you come across challenges on your way to achieving your goals.

I realised early on that I had a passion for personal development. I enjoy helping people and encouraging them to strive to achieve. I used to write career talks to present to student unions in my village. I also had a passion for public speaking from an early age. I remember leading the debating team in my secondary school in inter-school debates and winning prizes for our establishment. In secondary school, I was a mentor to my classmates who were struggling. I never turned anyone away because the more people I helped, the more confident I was. However, I lost these passions along the way and it has taken me several years to reconnect with them. But I'm happy that I have been able to do so. I don't believe that it's too late for me. So many people have lost their childhood passions and have never found them again and for some, sadly, their dreams died with them and are wasting in the grave. We will never know what great impact they would have had in their families, their communities and in our world if they had kept those dreams alive.

So, for many of you who might be thinking that it is too late, I would like to reassure you that it is never too late. As long as you are still breathing, I believe that you can still find your passion and make a difference in the world, in a way that only *you* could. There is nothing better to live for than what you are passionate about, your real purpose; something you would be happy to do for free if required and still enjoy it. What could that be for you? Find it!

Positive Thinking

"A man is literally what he thinks, his character being the complete sum of all his thoughts." – James Allen

The thoughts that we constantly dwell on determine our destiny. There is creative power in our thoughts and by using it, we can create a desirable future for ourselves. In the same vein, our lives will be a misery if we harbour negative thoughts. To achieve our dreams, we need to cultivate the skill of tuning our thoughts to the positive channel. Be optimistic about a solution no matter how bad the situation may be. It is possible! Believe it! One of the greatest obstacles to success is what we think about and how we utilise our thoughts. The good news is that we have absolute control over our thoughts and that means that we have absolute control of our fate in life.

I am reminded of when I first read the book, '*Think and Grow Rich*' by Napoleon Hill. It was simply transformational because although nothing had changed in my circumstance at the time, my view and interpretation of what was happening in my life changed and I could feel the innate creative power burning like a coal inside of me. I became very hopeful for the future, less stressed, less frustrated, and full of expectations for a better life. I was in touch with the biblical phrase about faith being the evidence of things hoped for. I could see a bright future very clearly and was excited to be alive and working towards that. Amazing!

The phenomenon called depression is simply a stream of negative thoughts based on negative interpretations of events happening in our lives. A negative mindset can never see anything positive in life even when things are going well. It is characterised by feelings of hopelessness, worthlessness, low self-esteem, gloominess, sickness, disaster, and failure. Can I just clarify that I am not suggesting that one must be always positive, enthusiastic, and driven? Life is not a straight line or a plain ride. Life is generally made up of ups and downs, highs, and lows, straight and crooked paths, hills, and valleys. Everyone experiences lows and highs sometimes no matter how positive or negative their mindsets are. However, it is your default mindset that is important here. If your predominant mindset is negative, you are more likely to dismiss good things happening in your life because you don't believe you deserve them. You are also more likely to always expect bad things to happen to confirm your belief that bad things always happen to you.

What is your predominant mindset? Do you know that you attract what you think about? This is the law of attraction and it is a universal law. Do you want to be rich? Then think about riches and do not dwell on poverty even though you might be poor now. Do you want to lose weight? Have a picture in your mind of the person you want to become and do not focus on the problem which is the weight you want to lose. Do you want to start a business? Just start and focus on the outcome you want from the business. Well, let me warn you that the fact that you are thinking about what you want does not mean that it is going to be a smooth ride to your goal. No, not at all. There are going to be obstacles and you will still have to put in the work. However, if you remain positive, focused, and persistent you will achieve your goals.

Positive Affirmations and Self-Talk Positive affirmations are an important aspect of self-motivation. What you say repeatedly will eventually reflect on who you have become. Sometimes because of our past experiences, backgrounds, and culture we have formed beliefs that are limiting our view of what is possible in our lives. At times, we wallow in self-pity as a result. You can apply positive affirmations to every aspect of your life - when you are feeling lonely, for example, or when you're experiencing stress or are overwhelmed by the pressures of life, or when you're facing financial difficulties.

Examples of positive affirmations are – 'I am a good person', 'Wonderful things are happening in my life', 'I am the head and not the tail', 'I forgive myself for all my past mistakes', 'I am the author of my destiny', 'I refuse to give up', 'I have faith that this will also come to pass', 'I love myself', 'I trust myself', 'Money is coming to me from different sources in a constant flow' and so on. These have the potential to lift your spirits when you feel down. You could even download positive affirmations audios or use CDs and listen to them regularly.

What do you repeatedly say about yourself? What do you say to yourself? Sometimes self-talk can be the best conversation you can ever have, if it is positive and self-motivating. I remember how nervous I was when I decided to go into public speaking. But I kept reassuring myself that I could do it. "*Manfred, come on, you can do it!*" I would say repeatedly. I would video myself presenting short talks and wondering if anyone would ever listen to them but I held onto the thought that if others were doing it I could do it, too.

I remember how nervous I felt when I posted some of those videos on Facebook and how reassured I was when I had some 'likes' and positive comments. But I was prepared to be vulnerable, to risk embarrassment and even humiliation so that I could grow. This should be your attitude when you are starting out. Do not let the fear of what people might think or say hold you back.

This is very useful, especially when people you trust are doubtful of your ability to achieve your goal and they are openly critical. Positive self-talk is like positive affirmations and serves the purpose of reassuring you that it is possible. You can have what you want. Positive affirmations and self-talk can re-focus your mind from the problems and help you to focus on the solutions.

Persistence:

"Energy and persistence conquer all things." Benjamin Franklin

Persistence is an attribute which allows you to continue to strive towards your goals despite the challenges and obstacles on the way. The journey to greatness is not a smooth ride. Obstacles are natural features on the expressway to achievement. They come in the form of criticism, opposition, financial difficulties, lack of resources, lack of certain skills, lack of connections and so forth.

These obstacles are not there to deter you, as many people appear to believe. Rather, they are there to build you up and cause you to grow. If only you could keep going, the obstacles would give way. Obstacles are like automatic doors, if you get close enough, they will open for you. It is a shame how many people do not go after their goals just because they know that there will be obstacles on the way.

There is a story about a man who set out to hew a huge piece of rock. Several strikes and there was no sign of any impact on the rock but he kept going until the two hundredth strike finally cracked the rock. Then a question was asked as to which strike was responsible for the rock cracking. You can answer it your own way based on your interpretation which will be determined by your predominant mindset, but I believe that *all* the strikes had a role to play in the outcome. If the man had stopped at the one hundred and ninety-ninth strike, he would have failed in his objective.

> **"A little persistence, a little more effort, and what seemed hopeless failure may turn to glorious success'"– Elbert Hubbard**

Patience:

"Patience is bitter, but its fruit is sweet." - Aristotle

Patience refers to the ability to accept or tolerate delay without expressing the emotions of anger and anxiety. This also implies the ability to endure difficult times and remain focused on your goals with an attitude that, 'this too shall pass'. This is a powerful attribute to have and it is essential for success in any endeavour.

Nature doesn't normally give us what we want, when we want it. There is usually a gap between planting and harvest time, which demands that we wait. Everyone who has engaged in agriculture or horticulture in whatever form can bear testament to this fact of nature. These people understand that they need to wait for the harvest after planting. Let us learn this great lesson from Nature itself. If you want to lose weight or develop a six-pack, it will not happen overnight. You need to identify a suitable weight-loss programme, develop a plan and start working on the plan. Then you need to be patient with yourself. Jumping on the scales after your first work-out is a good idea only if you want to record your baseline weight. However, you will probably notice some benefits after a week or more of engaging in the programme consistently and persistently.

Sadly, we live in an era where instant gratification has become the norm and many people are caught up in get-rich-quick euphoria - only to learn the hard way that patience is, indeed, golden, sometimes after they have lost everything. Scams are rife, beware! If it's too good to be true, it probably is. Do not fall for it.

I remember when Uber was floating its shares on the stock market in 2019. It was like a gold rush and I was conned by some people who promised great returns from the IPO. I lost £5000 because I got carried away and did not do my due diligence. This is just one of my many experiences. Please do your due diligence and be patient. Be warned!

> **"Patience, persistence and perspiration make an unbeatable combination for success."- Napoleon Hill**

Seasons come around in a cycle and if you do not like winter, there is nothing you can do about it. Winter will always follow autumn and summer will always follow spring and in that order. We cannot change that; it's just the way it is. Many people tend to waste precious energy in whining and moaning, even when they know that it is not within their power to change things. Impatience seems to have a grasp on people, leading to superficial success that will not stand the test of time. According to Saadi, "Have patience. All things are difficult before they become easy."

Positive Imagination

"The imagination is literally the workshop wherein are fashioned all the plans created by man. The impulse, the desire, is given shape, form, and action through the aid of the imaginative faculty of the mind."- Napoleon Hill

Practice the art of developing a picture of what you want in your mind. See yourself living the lifestyle you want, driving the car you want, living in the house that you want. There is a creative power in imagination.

Everything that is created was once in the imagination of the person who created it. They usually start by holding a picture in their mind and then go to work to produce it in a physical form. If you want something, create a clear picture in your mind and imagine yourself possessing that which you want. You could literally create a new future for yourself through the power of your imagination combined with a well-directed action plan, persistently executed.

> **"Imagination is more important than knowledge. For knowledge is limited to all we now know and understand, while imagination embraces the entire world, and all there ever will be to know and understand" – Albert Einstein**

As you can see, imagination has no boundaries. That is the power of your mind, a place of possibilities. Every human achievement was at one point only a thought in the mind of someone. Tap into this power to accelerate your progress. Anyone can develop this important skill through regular practice. Start *imagining* yourself into your desired goal or acquiring some great fortune.

Positive Adjustment Positive adjustment is a psychological concept which refers to an individual's state of mind and overall well-being in the context of their ability to adapt or cope effectively with changes in their environment. It measures things like self-esteem, stress levels, anxiety and depression. As you are probably aware, changing our lives for the better requires that we stretch outside our comfort zone. This demands that we raise our standards and step up our activities in every aspect of our lives relating to our goals. This can be a daunting thing to achieve unless we are very motivated. For example, someone who wants to lose weight, will need to engage in focused activity and a monitoring programme while working towards his/her goals. This process might require a complete change of direction and routine from what is normal for that individual and could be incredibly stressful and challenging.

You must have a positive attitude towards change as well as the process of change, otherwise you might lack the motivation to persist when you come across obstacles on the way. It is therefore important that you take ownership of the changes you want to see. Do not feel pressured to make changes, otherwise you might not follow through with them. Likewise, when you have achieved your goals, you might not be able to sustain or maintain them.

“When you can’t change the direction of the wind – adjust your sails.” - H. Jackson Brown Jr

Positive adjustment is essential for you to be able to cope with changes that you have no control over, and especially if you perceive those changes to be against your progress. Always remember that it is not what is happening around you but how you respond or react to it that determines the outcome. When management introduces new changes in the workplace, most people tend to be very resistant and try to block them. Stop asking, ‘Why are they doing this all the time, they don’t really care about us. Who do they think they are? But ask instead, ‘How can I use this situation to my advantage?’ There is always an advantage to be had in every change - pay careful attention and read between the lines.

Chapter Six

EXECUTION
(The P.I.P Triangle)

"It is hard to fail, but it is worse never to have tried to succeed. In this life we get nothing save by effort" – Theodore Roosevelt

Execution means to perform or carry out a plan. This requires that you actually do something and take some steps towards achieving your dreams. Execution is a sign that you are committed to the decision and that you are willing to get your hands dirty in order to realise your dreams.

In what I have tagged the 'P.I.P Triangle', I have presented the three elements of execution as Planning, Implement and Promote.

There are three elements to this:

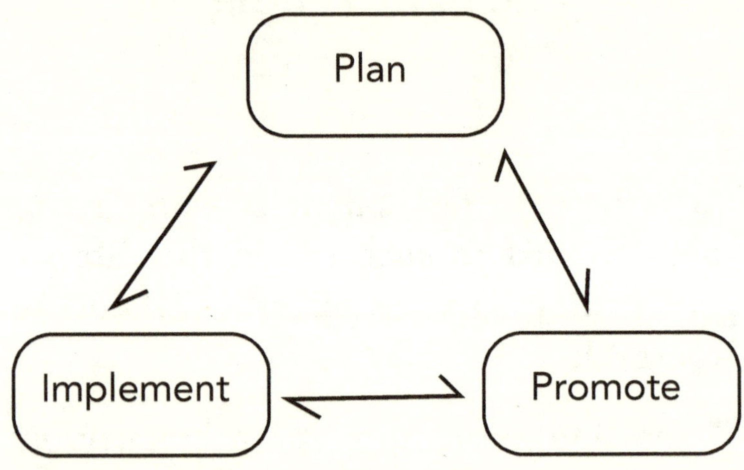

Plan

'He who fails to plan is planning to fail.' - Winston Churchill

Once you have identified your goals and defined them very clearly, you need a plan. You will need to draw up a plan stipulating the steps you are going to take to attain your goals. Determine first what you want to achieve - that is, your goals which are based on your dreams or expected outcomes. Treat this as a project and make your plan detailed but not ambiguous. In this book we are going to use a simple format for goal-setting as propounded by George T Doran - the **S.M.A.R.T formula:**

As this is rather a practical section, I suggest that before you go any further, you should go and get yourself a notepad. And as you are reading through this chapter, I recommend that you write down your goals following the S.M.A.R.T format. Pick one of your goals for now and then return to this chapter when writing your other goals.

Now let's go:

S-Specific -Be specific with what you want to achieve. Do not say, 'I want to lose weight'. Say, 'I want to lose 10 kilograms'.

M-Measurable – There must be a way of measuring your progress to determine if you are on tract or not. Is the strategy working? If it is not, how can you make it work for you? For example, using reliable scales, you should be able to measure your weight at regular intervals to determine your progress. I do not recommend daily but maybe weekly. Allow a reasonable gap between each measurement to give time for actual progress to be made.

A-Achievable or Attainable – The goal should be attainable or achievable within the timeframe set for it. For example, if your goal is to obtain a first-class degree in Economics, this is an achievable goal if you are prepared to put in the work. You see, in life if you expect more from life you should be prepared to give more. Remember the saying, 'To whom much is given, much is expected.' This is true. The further you wish to go, the more expensive the journey. But remember that there must clearly be a strategy or steps that need to be taken to achieve them. Spell these out clearly and what needs to be done by whom.

R-Realistic – Be realistic about what results are expected. For instance, losing 40 kg within a week seems unrealistic and unreasonable. If you wish to graduate with a first-class degree, your previous academic performance should give an indication whether this is realistic or not. An unrealistic goal may be counter-productive because you are likely to be discouraged if you are unable to achieve your goals despite trying so hard. On the other hand, if your goal is too easy to reach, it will not help you to stretch beyond your comfort zone and you are unlikely to grow as a result. Goals need to be challenging enough to stretch you and bring about growth but not so unreasonably hard that they are unattainable.

Time Related- There must be a timeframe. State when you expect to achieve the goals. For example, commit to losing 10kg by 30th June. Measure your achievements in terms of time frames and work towards them.

Your goals must be in writing and placed where you can see and read them at least once daily. In fact, nurses should find this process quite easy because they regularly follow this format writing care plans for their patients. However, they do it as part of their work routine and don't use it when they are making their own plans.

Strategy is key to planning and is essential for goal attainment. It stipulates step-by-step what needs to be done and how (the methods needed) to achieve our goals. It spells out what resources are required and what are available. Resource-allocation is an important aspect of formulating the strategy because resources are usually limited. You might have to start with very few resources at the beginning and increase them with time. But I must warn you that if you need to do something badly enough, do not wait until you are fully-equipped before you start. Waiting for the perfect conditions is a great stumbling block to starting anything and making progress. Never use it as an excuse to procrastinate.

> **"A vision without a strategy remains an illusion." - Lee Bolman**

An important part of any strategy is building your team and network. You will need to select your team carefully. You will probably need the help and guidance of other people such as a mentor or coach. Also, you may need the support of like-minded individuals, either in a forum or specialised community, who will share ideas and experiences with you and possibly provide other services too.

When I decided to become a public speaker, I joined the Professional Speakers Academy. This organisation was very useful in building my experience as a speaker, as I learnt a lot from the mistakes of others and also got others to evaluate my presentations. I was assigned a mentor in the Academy and she scrutinised and critiqued my presentations and gave me feedback, as well as the support and guidance that I needed to improve.

GOAL SETTING EXERCISE:

You can do this now before continuing or return to it after.

Using the S.M.A.R.T Model write down goals for the following areas of your life:

1. **Financial/Economics**
2. **Personal Development**

3. **Business/Career**
4. **Health/Wellbeing**
5. **Spiritual**
6. **Relationships**
7. **Contribution**

You must write these goals down. Just start writing and do not over-analyse. Make your goals big enough to motivate you. Read them at least twice daily - in the morning when you wake up and just before going to bed. Review and update your goals. Check that your actions are still consistent with your goals, then review your daily actions to align with your goals. If they are not, adjust them. Start with long-term goals (two to ten years) and then break these down to medium-term goals (one to two years) and short-term goals (up to one year). Short-term goals could range from one day, one week, one month, three months, six months, nine months up to one year. Keep it simple and straightforward.

GOAL-SETTING DEMONSTRATION:

This is only an example and is very simplified. You should adapt it to suit your personal circumstances. A one-page goal is ideal, but the maximum should be two pages.

MY HEALTH GOAL

GOAL: I need to lose 15kg in six months starting from the 1st of October to the 31st of March.

This means losing 2.5kg in one month.

Which means losing 0.625kg in 1 week.

(This is specific, measurable, achievable, realistic and within a time frame)

STRATEGY:

A. ACTION REQUIRED:

GYM

I will register with the gym.

I will get a personal trainer at the gym.

I will attend the gym three days a week (Mondays, Wednesdays, Fridays).

I will work out for at least two hours at each gym attendance.

HOME

I will go for a walk three days a week (Tuesdays, Thursdays, Saturdays).

I will walk for at least thirty minutes each day (or use the exercise bike instead).

I will reduce my normal food portions by half.

I will eat only a special diet for the first six weeks (if this is required, you will need a diet plan).

I will drink two litres of water/fluid every day (you will need a calibrated water bottle to monitor this).

I will not eat takeaway meals more than once a week.

OFFICE

I will stand up from my desk and walk around for at least one minute every hour.

I will take the stairs instead of the lift.

B. TOOLS/EQUIPMENT REQUIRED

Money to pay for gym membership.

Weighing scales.

Weight diary.

Pen.

Gym kit (clothes, trainers, water bottle, towel).

IMPLEMENT: ACTION! ACTION!! ACTION!!!

Do what you have planned to do.

Just take the action.

Push yourself.

Remain focused and determined.

REVIEW/MONITORING:

I will check my weight once a week (every Sunday morning).

I will record my weight in my weight diary.

I will change my plan if my target weight is not met (this could mean increasing work-out time, eating less food or being more committed to the plan if you were behind).

Whenever you meet or exceed your target, celebrate by treating yourself (not indulging

yourself). This will build your confidence that you are making progress. Don't wait until the final target is met before you celebrate - the weekly targets should also be celebrated.

IMPLEMENT

> **"A good plan implemented today is better than a perfect plan implemented tomorrow." - George Patton**

Implementing means taking the actions necessary to achieve our goals. The whole point of having a dream is doing whatever is necessary to bring it to realisation. Irrespective of how brilliant an idea is, without action it cannot be born and therefore has no chance of being alive in the world. Everything ever created has been because of someone daring to act on their ideas. The farmer who hopes for a harvest is the farmer who has taken the time to plant his crops in due season; the one who plants nothing can expect to get nothing.

> **"The universe doesn't give you what you ask for with your thoughts; it gives you what you demand with your actions." – Steve Maraboli**

Action leads to progress or productivity and massive action leads to massive success. The bigger your dreams, the bigger the action required to achieve them. Just keep going with your eyes on the outcome. In the interim, it might appear as though nothing is happening, but just keep doing what you need to do. Remember the story of the man hewing the stone I shared earlier? Every strike matters!

Like an Olympic athlete you need to focus on Gold. You need to challenge yourself. Give it your best shot. Give it your all! As a salesman, just keep going despite the rejections - increase your calls. As an employee, give more than you are paid to do. If you want to lose weight, follow your plans even when you do not feel like it. Do not look for excuses to stop even when it is painful. Remember there is no gain without pain. After the pains will come the pleasure, the celebration, the victory.

> **"If you really want to do something, you'll find a way. If you don't, you'll find an excuse." – Jim Rohn**

Most people do not take the actions necessary to achieve their goals because of fear and lack of confidence. This could involve a fear of rejection, embarrassment, humiliation or losing face. Acting requires courage and bravery. And courage does not mean absence of fear but being able to act despite the fear you are feeling. Do you think the soldiers who fight in battles are not afraid? Do you think fire-fighters who confront fires to rescue others are not afraid? Do you believe that parachutists or skydivers are not scared? These people are usually afraid, but they act *despite* their fears because they have extraordinarily strong reasons to do so. They have a passion for what they do and they feel a sense of obligation or duty. You also need to have this mindset if your goals are important to you. You will need to do whatever it takes to ensure you achieve them despite the fear and anxiety you might be feeling.

Another reason people do not take the action they need to is because of their perceived pain and gain from the action itself or the outcome. We act because of either desiring to move away from pain or to move towards gain or pleasure. I heard someone use the following example - he visited a friend and his dog was sitting in the corner whimpering and groaning. When he asked the man why the dog was engaged in that behaviour, he replied that the dog was sitting on a nail. When asked why the dog did not get off the nail, he replied that the dog probably did not feel that it was hurting enough!

> **"The secret of success is learning how to use pain and pleasure instead of having pain and pleasure use you. If you do that, you're in control of your life. If you don't, life controls you." – Anthony Robbins**

Our perception of pain and pleasure could be the propelling force for our action. Generally, if the sense of pain is more that the perceived pleasure from taking action, we refrain from acting. Consider someone who needs to lose weight. They know that losing weight is good for them and that it will make them feel better, fitter, healthier and more confident. However, they refuse to act because of the potential pain of going on a diet and denying themselves the pleasure of food as well as giving themselves the pain and the inconvenience of embarking on an exercise programme. If, in their mind, the perceived pain is greater than the benefit, they will not take action. Most people will not act until they reach breaking point. This is the point of disgust where they can no longer stand the pain associated with their condition, where they say to themselves, 'I've had it'. On the other hand, if they feel that the sense of pleasure the outcome will bring him is greater than the pain, they are more likely to take the action required to bring about the desired change. Sometimes it takes something drastic to get to this point like an embarrassment or humiliation, for example.

"What you do speaks so loud that I cannot hear what you say"– Ralph Waldo Emerson

PROMOTE:

"Success is not final, failure is not fatal: it is the courage to continue that counts." Winston Churchill

Promotion means increasing public awareness of a person, product, or organisation. As an individual who is driven by purpose and goals, you are positioning yourself as an authority. For example, if you have been struggling to lose weight and you eventually have a breakthrough by following a well thought-out plan, you have positioned yourself as an expert in that area and will now be able to guide other people with similar problems to find their own breakthroughs.

The point I am making here is that when you have a plan and have acted on that plan, even if you initially appeared to have failed to achieve your goals, you have not really failed unless you decide to quit. In the process of enforcing your plans, you should have learnt some lessons that could benefit other people trying to do what you have done. Of course, those lessons should equip you to make necessary changes that could help you to grow and be successful. And better still if you are successful, you are well-placed to support others to do the same.

> **"Success does not lie in results but in efforts, Being the best is not so important, doing the best is all that matters." - Unknown**

Chapter Seven

REVIEW
(The E.E.G Model)

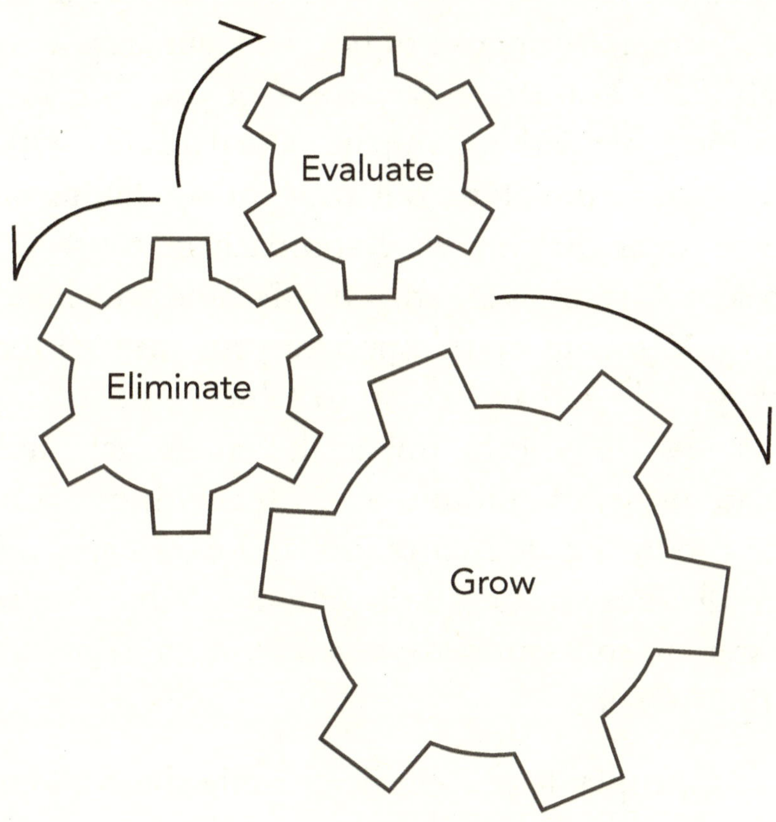

Evaluate your progress

"Evaluate what you want ... because what gets measured, gets produced." - James A. Belasco

Evaluation is the process of measuring an actual result to see if it meets the desired or expected outcome. It is a key process in determining if we have attained our goals or not. I encourage you to habitually evaluate every aspect of your life and business regularly. Compare actual results with expected results. Find out why you are failing in some areas. Review your approach or strategies to see which ones are still effective and which are not. Do this in every aspect of your life and for every goal you have set out to achieve - including business, physical, financial, emotional and relationships. Continue to do those things that are producing desired results and eliminate and change those strategies that are not. Subject your system to constant review with a view to constant improvement.

Most people live their lives aimlessly without stopping regularly to take stock. This is because they have no goals or else their goals are lousy and uninspiring. A meaningful evaluation can only happen when there is clarity about what you have set out to achieve. It is an audit of performance or results in order to compare the expected against the actual outcome. It might also involve an evaluation of your relationships because the people you associate with can determine whether you achieve your goals in life or not.

In healthcare we call it, 'reflective practice' and it involves a review of what has been helpful and what has not, especially when an untoward incident has occurred. It usually helps us to learn lessons that can be applied in future to manage similar incidents in a more efficient and effective way by avoiding what did not work well in previous episodes.

> **"Evaluate the people in your life. It's time to promote, demote, or terminate. You are the CEO of your life!" - Tony A Gaskins Jr**

Evaluation should be an on-going process. You do not need to wait until the result before carrying out a review, it should be a regular occurrence. For example, let us assume that the goal of a Premier League football team is to win the trophy. Review should happen during and after each match to determine what has worked well, what has not worked well, where the weakness is and so on. This is why some players are replaced during a match. Effective evaluation will help the team management to formulate a strategy to remedy what has not been helpful - this might mean changing tactics or players or offering psychological support to some players, for example.

Eliminate strategies that are not working. The process is like the act of pruning a plant to allow new growth. Do not be afraid to make changes when necessary. This can be a remarkably simple procedure or a daunting task and might require courage to take the required action to effect the changes needed. As a leader, you need to be brave and courageous enough to say, 'I think this isn't working, let us try something else'. It could mean letting someone go, changing a process, ending a contract with a supplier or customer, changing a method or a piece of equipment or amending a policy. Being proactive is essential in determining what requires changing before they affect the final outcome, and this can make the difference between success and failure.

> **"Deciding what not to do is as important as deciding what to do." – Steve Jobs**

Grow:

> **"Without continual growth and progress, such words as improvement, achievement, and success have no meaning." - Benjamin Franklin**

Growth comes from making changes and being flexible. The world is changing fast especially with technological advancement. What worked yesterday might not work today. Be flexible, willing, and brave enough to make essential adjustments to stimulate growth in every aspect of your life. Always seek to improve yourself, your health, your profit, your customers, and your people (staff) and your business will grow.

Be flexible and embrace new ideas when necessary. Be willing to invest in new technology to improve your processes. Be prepared to seize new opportunities in the marketplace to your advantage.

However, growth must be controlled and professionally managed. For a new and small business, rapid growth and uncontrolled expansion can be detrimental to the health of the company with negative repercussions both in the short and long term. Business expenses could grow astronomically compared to revenues and this could set the company back. Employees could be stressed out due to their additional workload and resources could be over-stretched because of unprecedented growth within a short period of time. The same is applicable to personal growth in every aspect of your private life.

Chapter Eight

SUCCESS
(The W.I.N.G Factor)

Success means different things to different people. It is usually embodied in the result but whatever it means to you, it is the reward for the daily efforts or actions and commitment to the achievement of your set goals. Success is not always about achieving big things and it might be the little things that eventually add up to the goal. For someone who wants to lose weight, for instance, success might mean reaching their target weight or making progress towards reaching their target weight by consistent effort. For a businessman, success might mean reaching the target profit. This would only be possible by focusing on the quality of your product or service on a daily basis and ensuring that each customer experiences real value for money and satisfaction.

You must have a way of measuring or determining your own success. Clearly defined goals can give you clarity as to how you are progressing towards them and will leave you in no doubt about when you have achieved them.

Win and celebrate Whenever we achieve something, especially a major goal, we should pat ourselves on the back. Also, congratulate yourself for the small, daily signs of progress, or the milestones reached.

> **"Self-congratulation is a sign of maturity but demanding congratulation is a sign of immaturity." – Jim Rohn**

Celebrating yourself when you have achieved something can boost your confidence and inspire you to press on to achieve greater goals. Celebration can take various forms. It can be with yourself alone or with your family or a team. It could be just getting excited, like when your football team scores a goal, or perhaps giving yourself a treat or even taking a luxury holiday. Celebration is better and sweeter when it is instant or soon after the goal has been achieved. This indicates that the celebration is tied to that goal. For instance, a football team celebrates every goal scored while the match is still in progress. They don't wait until the end of the match to rejoice. Finally, at the end of the match, there is a grand celebration if the team emerges victorious. Winning a trophy is a different level of celebration. This should be our attitude in celebrating our success.

Innovate: Success is not a permanent state or condition. Any condition is subject to change, so we need to guard our success zealously otherwise we lose it. When the crops are yielding, do not just fold your arms otherwise the weeds might take over your fields! The irony of life is that there is always room for improvement.

> **"We cannot solve our problems with the same thinking we used when we created them." – Albert Einstein**

Remember that you can always better your best. So, keep asking the question, 'What can I improve? What can we do better? You need to continuously innovate to remain relevant in the marketplace, especially in these fast-moving times. This is important for businesses as well as individuals. The world is changing fast. New technologies are being developed every day that are changing how we communicate and how we do things. This is the reality of life and we just must plug into it. Technology is there to serve us and not to stop us.

> **"Innovation distinguishes a leader and a follower" – Steve Jobs**

Nurture your success base: Nurture your people, customers, and support system. Life is a game and successes are mostly teamwork. Nurturing your team means developing or uplifting them and when people feel appreciated, they tend to be more committed. This is a mark of good leadership. This is as important in business as it is in our personal life and relationships.

> **"Even if it is for one second, appreciate those who go the extra mile to make you happy. These are the priceless things in life." – Toni Payne**

Acknowledge those who have contributed, even in a ridiculously small measure, to your success. This could be just a word of encouragement or appreciation, a referral, or just saying 'Thank you.' Do not forget your network and support system;

you could not have done it all alone. Showing appreciation to members of your support network will strengthen your relationship with them and could cause them to do more to support you in future. It is arrogant to think that you have got to where you are all by yourself.

Give Back

"There is no happiness in having or in getting, but only in giving." – Henry Drummond

When you become successful, do not forget the need for social contribution. Remember it is more blessed to give than to receive. I believe that we are blessed to give a blessing. So, give your time, money, materials, share your knowledge, experience, resources. Giving is like pruning a tree and refreshing its ability to be more fruitful.

"When you cease to make a contribution, you begin to die" – Eleanor Roosevelt.

Giving is living, it is a noble act that can bring us true happiness and a sense of fulfilment. Hanging onto your wealth and not giving back is like taking a deep breath and holding it. This can only lead to breathlessness and then gasping for air. So be generous with your resources and make a difference in the world. Remember that in the words of Benjamin Franklin, "*The use of money is all the advantage there is in having it.*"

Please note that you do not need to wait until you have achieved everything you have set your mind on before you give. Make giving a part of your life journey. Everyone has something that someone else needs to thrive at any point in time. Giving opens doors for more breakthroughs.

About The Author

Manfred Gwunireama is a Nigerian-born, British public speaker, coach, mentor, trainer, teacher and entrepreneur with a passion for personal development and mental wellbeing. He is the founder of mindzemancipation.com, an organisation created to provide information, training and coaching through online courses, seminars and workshops. He aims to inspire people, challenge their limiting beliefs and help them to re-invent themselves, take back control of their lives and transform their destinies.

He is the creator of The D.R.E.A.M.E.R.S SUCCESS PLATFORM which is a training and coaching programme for helping people re-evaluate where they are, where they want to be and looking at how to get from where they are to where they want to be.

Manfred has worked extensively as a psychiatric nurse in several mental health hospitals and units, both within the NHS and private sector in the United Kingdom, and has extensive experience in guiding very distressed patients on their individual journeys to recovery. This work has opened his eyes to the reality of psychiatric conditions and the impact that our negative beliefs, attitude, lifestyle and relationships have on mental health. He has a passion for helping people overcome difficulties through challenging, debunking and replacing their limiting beliefs. Showing them how to transform their thoughts and shift their paradigms, he helps people to re-invent themselves, regain self-confidence and take back control of their lives.

Manfred lives in London, in the United Kingdom with his family. He is happily married to his wife, Thelma, and has two lovely daughters Precious, aged eleven, and Michelle, aged seven.

www.ingramcontent.com/pod-product-compliance
Lightning Source LLC
LaVergne TN
LVHW091005080826
845145LV00003B/1139

* 9 7 8 1 9 9 9 6 6 4 2 7 5 *